MEGA
CARS

picthall and gunzi

Created & produced by:
Picthall & Gunzi Limited
21A Widmore Road
Bromley
Kent BR1 1RW
United Kingdom

Copyright © 2007 Picthall & Gunzi Limited

Designer: Paul Calver
Written and edited by: Christiane Gunzi
Editorial assistant: Katy Rayner
Vehicle consultant: Gary Boyd-Hope

Hardback ISBN **978-1-905503-17-9**

Reproduction in Singapore by Colourscan
Printed & bound in China by WKT Company Ltd

**Picthall & Gunzi would like to thank the following
companies and individuals for the use of their images:**
A Touch of Class Limousines; Alamy; Ariel Motor Company
Ltd; Bauer-Millett; Jamie Bell; F. Belley www.PhotoF1.com;
Glynne Bowsher; Bugatti Automobiles SAS; Caterpillar;
Chrysler Group; DaimlerChrysler UK; DCUK Marketing
Archive; Ford Motor Company; Steve Bailey, Gibbs
Technologies; Simon Jagassar; Dave Jones at Santa
Pod Raceway; Koenigsegg; Lamborghini; Land Rover;
newlaunches.com; Robin Richardson; Rolls-Royce Motor
Cars; Mark Sims rallygallery.com; Truck Customs by
Chris www.f650pickups.com; Volkswagen Group UK Ltd.

BIGFOOT® is a registered trademark of BIGFOOT 4x4, Inc.
Hazelwood, MO, USA. ©2007. All rights reserved.

Monster Truck photos provided by Matt Jorgensen.

Photograph of Morgan AeroMax reproduced with kind
permission of David Smith.

Picthall and Gunzi would like to thank Kenneth D. Ringold
for the kind permission to use the images of Hot Rods on
pages 14 and 15.

Please note that every effort has been made to check the
accuracy of the information contained in this book, and
to credit the copyright holders correctly. Picthall & Gunzi
apologise for any unintentional errors or omissions, and
would be happy to include revisions to content and/or
acknowledgments in subsequent editions of this book.

CONTENTS

Sports Cars 4

Dragsters and Hot Rods 14

Movie Cars 24

Supercars 6

Four-by-Fours 16

Classic Cars 26

Luxury Cars 8

Pick-ups 18

Super-fast Cars 28

Race and Rally Cars 10

Monster Trucks 20

Cars of the Future 30

Formula One Cars 12

Fun Cars 22

Let's Match! 32

SPORTS CARS

These fast, exciting cars are sports cars. They are low on the ground and they have space for two people. The Lamborghini Murciélago is named after a Spanish bull that was famous for being brave and strong. Sports cars cost a lot of money.

Ferrari F430

Ferrari
This Italian car has a gearbox like Formula One racing cars, so the driver can change gears very quickly.

Lamborghini
This sports car has a top speed of 211 miles an hour. It has long wing mirrors which can fold in and out.

Inside a Lamborghini

low body

Porsche 911 GT3

rear spoiler

Porsche

This German car can go from 0 to 60 miles an hour in four seconds. It has excellent brakes, so it can stop suddenly when it needs to.

Which sports car is named after a famous bull?

folding mirror

protective steel door

Lamborghini Murciélago

A good grip

Jeeps, Land Rovers and Hummers have powerful engines. They can drive over rocks, mud, ice and snow and up steep mountain tracks without sliding about.

Jeep
Commander

heated
windscreen

Hummer H2

electric
windows

Land
Rover

PICK-UPS

These big, powerful pick-up trucks are used by farmers and builders to do tough jobs. They can carry heavy loads and tow other vehicles. People also like to use pick-up trucks because they are fun to drive.

exhaust

Ford F750

tow hook

Ford F650

This Ford pick-up has a 300 horsepower engine. Some Fords have a special camera to help the driver see behind the vehicle when it is towing things.

light

grip

Ford F650

tough tyres

aluminium step

Dodge Ram

This fast pick-up can go from 0 to 60 miles an hour in five seconds. Its top speed is 154 miles an hour and it has a 500 horsepower engine.

Dodge Ram SRT-10

aluminium wheel

bumper

Which pick-up is called the Dodge M80?

Ford F950

Can you point to?

exhaust   wing mirror   wheel arch

Dodge M80

Dodge M80

This cool pick-up looks like a truck from the 1930s. It is strong and it has five gears. Dodge pick-ups are tough machines and can drive over rough ground.

MONSTER TRUCKS

About 30 years ago, a few people decided to make their pick-ups look more exciting. They added huge wheels and their trucks were called "monster trucks". Now millions of people watch these mega vehicles race and do displays at shows.

Can you point to?

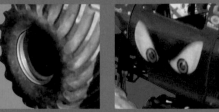

tyre   eyes   teeth

Bigfoot

The owner of the first monster truck, "Bigfoot", added huge tyres to his Ford truck then drove over some old cars in a field for fun.

Clever tricks

Drivers make their trucks do jumps. Some spin their truck in a circle. This is called a "doughnut".

"Monstrous"

Which was the first monster truck?

"Swamp Thing"

Car crusher

Monster trucks race each other, jump and crush other vehicles by driving over them. They have special switches that turn off the engine if the driver loses control.

"Slingshot"

old cars

"Bigfoot"

pick-up truck

mega tyre